The Fortune of a Fairy

Margot White

Children of Avalon

Margot White Music

www.margotwhite official.com
© 2020 by Margot White
All rights reserved.

Published 2019, 2020
Printed in United Kingdom and
United States of America

ISBN 13: 978-0-9845474-4-9 (PBK)

Illustrations by Bárbara Malagoli http://
www.barbaramalagoli.com/
@bmalagoli

Contents

7	Acknowledgements
10	Flame of Arcady
11	alice
12	alice ii
13	Silent
14	Sister
16	Did you doubt…
19	August . 21 . The Morning
20	August . 21 . The Evening
21	August . 22
22	Translation
23	Selenite / A Paris Flower
24	Pisces Moon
25	Coal Room
26	Friday Skin
27	15 Trois Rivières 1953 15 ml
28	Helios + Ra
29	Cygnet
30	Lava Lamp
31	Stonehenge Three : Mother, Daughter, Aunt]

32	Orchid Wheel
33	Prince
34	Lucky Horse
35	Astral House
36	The Novel
38	Let Be
39	Dizzy and Such
40	Mephistopheles
42	Chimera
43	New Year Eve
44	Teeth of Kore
45	Chalice of Artemis
46	Kaleidoscope at 1.33 AM
47	Sister Poppy
48	The Gift of Snow
49	Echo Country
50	Electric Wolf
51	La Belle au bois dormant
52	Rorschach
53	I'm Your Alien
54	Ondine

56	Child of a Psychic
57	Not Quite Eight
58	Mind
59	Black Cabinet
60	Six
61	Moth
62	Gypsy Boy of the Darro
63	Inverness
64	Bodies of Storm
65	Cosmo Flora
66	Duel
67	Work
68	Hothouse Flower
69	Kataware — doki
70	Naked in the Spaniard Inn
71	oh, Croatia
72	Carte Blanche
73	Tangerine Oak
75	Ode to Sensitives
76	Witch
77	Wolfish

Acknowledgments

I would like to thank the following for contributing to this body of work. Without you, the inspiration filling this book would be mere vapours.

Illustrations by Bárbara Malagoli
http://www.barbaramalagoli.com/
@bmalagoli

My family and ancestors. Don Weidemann, Marianne Weidemann, Jamie Weidemann, Maya Weidemann, Kae McLaughlin, Sheryl and Bruce Cox, Ralph and Billye McLaughlin, Don Sr. and LaVerne Weidemann, Gail King, Julie and Marty Payeur, Craig Weidemann, Kris Clark, Scott and Mary Kae McLaughlin and the rest of the roots on both sides.

Dearest friends. Shakti Miller, Terry Sherrell, Katie Copeland and everyone in Venice Beach, David Thornley, the Thornley Family, Emily Cippele, Mallory Pickrell, Alice Ancient, Kayleigh 'Moon Child', Eleanor Roberts, Alex, Robert, Megan and the magical Lane women, Rosalie Miller, Ada Smith, Jennifer Leiva, Rebecca Ruiz, 'Mama' Jen, Ryan Marks, Mark New, Casey, Michael White, Kathy Pearce, Marissa Stakowski, Mina Alchokeil, Heather Freed, Andrew Manley, Cami Alvarez, Les Best, Judahfi, everyone at 61 Stanhope in Brooklyn, the Raymond Family, tall Paul, Walter, AWAL, Francesco Marseglia, Sonia Shahid, Victoria Carr, Melanie Xulu, Helgi's, the rest of the Cherrywood Family, the Electric Church, Sun at Night, and every being who ever took a chance on me in my moments of experimentation. Also the Beatles. The list goes on and on, and if my very human awareness has neglected your name in this inclusion, please understand your impact has not gone unnoticed in my heart.

To all of the writers who have inspired my work. One day I will follow in the footsteps of Henry Miller and write a true story chronicling, with adequate detail, this trail, but until then may your spirits rejoice knowing you have helped me immeasurably on my path.

The Fortune of a Fairy

Flame of Arcady

There is a fire burns in Arcady
it burns for you, and it burns for me,
masterful scarlet, dried hands on maiden smocks
knows neither tear nor stain,
greets linen of lilies overwhelmingly
with restrain.

There is a fire burns in Arcady
it sounds of falling stars,
inexorable allure, it soothes and strains
beckons floating fleet,
onward to trod to meet
melody painted ivy faces pinned on forest walls.

There is a fire burns in Arcady, I see it in my mind.
Implacable serenity, crosses courseways
and all signs,
answering to none but itself.

alice

Alice asks me what that dagger is doing in my womb with a blade
    reflecting moonlight,
scarlet starts to bloom
I query at the mirror, absorbed by what I see somewhere in its
    realm I hear another part of me.
The chandelier is shining,
the room perambulates
magnetized by voices resounding from the well.

The frames are gold around me, the faces saccharine, The women
    in the paintings on the walls stare
at something I don't yet see.

Things that cease to be are just the phoenix of the ash.
Birds from other worlds
that someday we will see.

Galloping pathways furrowed in my mind, golden key in hand,
    curiosity my bird.
I bid farewell familiar
worlds, favor brilliancy
I cast off memories, stale clothing to the sea
let the seams and stitches loose the finer things.

alice ii

I suppose I'd like to know
what to do exactly with this feeling.
A flame caught itself
all tangled in my lips now,
is it some message from a future I walk toward
is it the ache people feel when they have lost a love that wasn't
  true.
Still I pretend the window I kissed wasn't frozen blue. I put one
  foot before the other and walk away.
I was headed home, some nights I go,
sometimes my feet confuse me,
ringing the bell of a Russian Jack, ack, ck, k.

Yes, you know him well I suppose.
He sets his stories on the rims of wineglasses He says, wear that
  necklace, nothing else.

Yet, I've decided to try this whole thing on alone, I like to feel the
  slicing air
when I learn these lessons
on these two feet.

I am able to say they are my own.

Though there are days when I feel a little nervous, and when Alice
  asks me how I feel
I stutter, the dagger in my womb is not yet gone it turns so slow
as though the moonlight grazing her window
is the key unlocking a memory.

Silent

Your first breath mimics the stars
I owe it for you to know me,
the troubled sense, it senses all things we took with us into the
    flight.
Silent, I like to think of a fireplace charming the room,
and the glass thats reflects it,
is another world waiting in the wings, or just asleep within.
A constant conversation, that's no way to live.
Is the rhythm of the heart enough for your desires, pricking at your
    bruises full of moonlight, shadowed by the trees reaching in
    from outside.
Silent beats
the deepest heart
still waters run the same.
I think I can hear you
in the library now
the books catch my fingers
there is no sound
except for your breathing
press my ear to the wall
what are you feeling on the other side.

Sister

It's true
I expect a great deal from the shoots of leaves, reliable as maps
to guide me within.
Sister, lift the veil around your heart Sister, too long we've been
    apart. Shadows of the world may frighten
I need your strength to make it brighter.
We are being born in a new world,
things impossible before are now possible. Blake, dry your tears,
your Mother wants you well enough
to gaze upon the sunrise.
Biblical leaves crumbling,
cast aside in favour of sacred being, release the proper eyes
to really see.
Sister, lift the veil around your heart, Sister, too long we've been
    apart. Shadows of the world may frighten
I need your strength to make it brighter.
Unraveling knots I always longed to see, her fingers danced across
    the string, sisters in a cool lamplight
Pinkie Swear forever
your secret in my heart.
Aching sometimes in between, growing pains is what they say,
    Blessed of all Women,
is her place.
Sister, lift the veil around your heart Sister, too long we've been
    apart. Shadows of the world may frighten
I need your strength to make it brighter.

Did you doubt...

my love. Her tearsong surged forth.
It seemed the same restless melody played every night, and every
    one of Tennyson's poems
rent her heart to remember its own
written in the grace of love,
the startled breath of mornings in love,
a summer bath and candlelit,
where surprises would be left to sit
and wait for their unending eyes
ablaze beneath a
Universal sky.
Though her pain it grew very great,
grew very tremendous, though
she knew with time it would pass—
a little less sure of this she seemed each day— or else it
    threatened forever to last, backwards and forwards it shook her
    soul until she could take no more,
she cried out to the Heavens, Have mercy, even this score.
Immediately the sky furiously blushed and all the autumn magpies
    hushed, two clouds peeled like parting hands and before her
    now there stood a man— though not a man of mortal hue,
his eyes a sage forgotten blue
his skin a silken shadow shimm'ring. He came to her in faerie
    clearing,
Are you asking what I think you ask, his tone curt and coy and
    mournful, like a puzzle ill fit to play.
There was a strangeness in him,
of what she could not describe.
It took all her strength to silently nod, to silently plead Heartache
    away,

I can make it so, and easily,
you won't remember him,
you won't remember a thing.
His words struck as if to stun
and bruised a softness where love had once won, could she believe
    he meant these words,
so casually tossed, so briefly spelled, would that be his remedy
some Circean flowered amnesia,
Yet as her horror grew at such thought
a blinding pang nailed all the more brightly,
if I should suffer but one day more
I will in truth shift beyond my recognised form,
So she hung her head, not with shame, but as deterrent from any
    game
her mind might make to play with her what is done, done, I own
    what I incur, she stated plain for all to hear,
If Life is here for us to live
and love and heartache part of life
I'll step once more in darkness,
for in darkness love came to me,
and into darkness it has gone
and in between there is Light I find,
and if curiosity is what will break these binds, I commit to forget
    his name,
for true love is stronger than any spell cast
so either freedom or true love—but not Heartache—will last.

August . 21 . The Morning

The rich, ruby, raw red pulsing exploding a thousand tiny points,
    stars from my veins. Beckoned by the cool air of her towering
    pillars. A refuge from August haze, yet
it is a surprising haven, in that
I had no idea the still wonder awaiting. It is
this exact sense which sets me to the pen It is the only thing
that will abate me
when I am in
a city
as sensuous
as Paris.
Beckoning me inside, mollifying
fiery, afflicted senses with its own peaceable urgings
This sort of beckoning comes from another place altogether.
    And what sweet privilege to be in relationship with Her most
    beautiful magic, I finger paint
a doorway across my hips.

August . 21 . The Evening

The clothes, the food, the baths, the perfume, the nighttime, the daytime, the notebooks and cafes, the jazz played in Châtelet, and St. Germain and the Tower, and the boys, and the freedom like a swallow airing her foundation in the sky.

August . 22

The bridge it is so high, so narrow, arcing above a slender body of water. The ember glowing windows smudge a whispering sky streaked by haunting blues, pinks, purples. It is this last shade, the question of its true body, its true art that draws me near. Paris is a well worded remedy for a broken heart. Its searing wounds cast by its singular beauty, transient as the moments spent by the Seine, fading as quickly as the sun behind a disguise of arcing ivory edifice, poplar notes rising and falling against the lives of the sky. The emotion it evokes is the only medicine strong enough for this loss. Now I know. Now I know heartbreak, and I know I will live through its wounds. Smoke rises then fades off another bridge, smaller, sloping just east and the air is as gentle as a kiss.

Translation

There is nothing that can be done, for this suffering is already in
 translation.
The symphony of the cosmos wears it like a necklace from the sea,
 still tasting of salt.
Like a gentle washing, I want to struggle with it fragile, frail
 struggle, throbbing like
the pulse of a sleeping lion
crying into his dreams,
prowling the whole of his desperation, into that far off never never
 land. Never the land, never is that land,
fading into distant sunsets
for all of the sunsets, existing in the transience of their work.

Selenite / A Paris Flower

You act as if I were wrong to want the moon.
In truth it was the moon who tried for me,
All I did, every night
was let her see
the better part of me.

Credulous tyrant rack my breast for that weak
breaking bone
Not my home
Somewhere deep inside of me

So I go to that wall writ by old,
Ages past
Swallow its fount
A dangerous
thing of glass

You act as if I were wrong
to want the moon,
but in truth it was the moon who begged for me,
All I did, every night
was let her see the better part of me.

Pisces Moon

Hadn't slept all night
So I surrendered to the dream
More real than life was
You standing in front of me
I was playing the piano
couldn't figure you out
the look on your face
Was of a different place
So I kept on
playing my heart out.

Coal Room

And you try to think, but the
dressing room is a grave
and all the people here, they look the same
Don't get too busy in your mind,
nothing there to help.

When all the world, with its very many ways,
denies the truth of your heart

Making it easy, it's not so hard to do,
the tower by the park
you forgot the miner's curfew
and you got left, coal on your cheeks
streaks to speak for the tunnels

Friday Skin

Baby, Leave the group at the table
we can go down the street
to a little spot I know
pressed between the man
with the top hat
and the falling cedar

sweetly sway under its Knowledge
past a block black row of Kensington flats
I don't have to go so soon,
only, let me know

Aquarius sensibility frames
the aqueduct of a season's
invincibility
Nevermind the
sensuality left fighting in the dust.

Grabbed us by the cuffs he did, He is
crazy for the time of day,
that coin means more to him than you
or me.

Here we are, pressed between
a fading summer sleep
a little love repeated
but fraying the edges
making out like little souls
so gentle, they take a little while to let on
they might feel worn

Trois Rivières 1953 25ml

your golden hair spilled down
Across a wilful gown you chose for his Rose
    you don't know anymore
if You want to wait
Still I hear You say hold on,
I won't be your chaser

You lost your Self in politics and clubs of sticks
and You bet your ideas on wine and cards
    like flowers set in stone

true that You are ivy quick
a cultured Gothic trimmed
by rogues between the bars of lords

You practice what You preach
A stranger's tomb is Feast
For all Your pages clad in Noble guests

out of the Dogs and men,
Your storm it crawls within
the chasms built by silver-set,

and You, wait for my mouth to react
my words are tied silk knot under teeth
Guilty with or without
how could I say a word.

Helios + Ra

How the rails of all the trains
wove a web like spidery rays
cost me nothing to weigh such threads
against the lead in my Sunday head

Cygnet

Because, of course, where did
the endless come from
lifting swarm of rider's hilt
barren but for its
friendship, its limitless fire
in body, that clear astral body

                      Her huge gaping eyes

Lava Lamp

I swivel in Spirit of your table
its pedestal quite like
my own silhouette
I wonder if
your ankle finds it so.

Blessed echo, redeeming sapphire, patterns
of life, tricolour drift
under wisdom of disco ball
distracting all East London backrooms

I am colder with my
coat on
than I am
without

I guess we are just two hearts of lava making love in a lamp.

Stonehenge Three : Mother, Daughter, Aunt

Train waves, hands of my heart,
weaving, gathering sending life in full
spirit,
who dives deep, plunging reckless hands
into the well,
the waters sacred and plentiful for all
who go to her,
seeking remonstrance, guidance, shelter,
wisdom, watchful, but above all,
this cool compassion
or warm in winter fashion,
whatever you need, She is that.

sparkling life-rife vapours anew,
to tend to luminous sinews of
ardent heart

Suppose you start to watch in this moment
the giving flame glowing
circumference abounding
a ripple, a ring
un-bounded Vision.

Orchid Wheel

A wondrous heart, she
blooms to feel, orchid on a velvet wheel
born with age-old wound to heal,
orchid on a velvet wheel.

At the fair she spins
on a coat she is pinned,
potable water within reveals,
the orchid on a velvet wheel.

Bowing in the blowing wind
an orchid picked by velvet hand,
top to bottom begin again,
the orchid picked by velvet hand.

Anticipation curves her neck,
her silken skin grows lover's breath,
petal thin she runs like sand,
the orchid picked by velvet hand.

Passion aroused a thousand hearts
orchid of the dancing dark,
vanishing leap, mist and spark
orchid of the dancing dark.

Climbs peculiar, feral and rampant
against estimate of aberrations,
and now a winsome light reveals
orchid on a velvet wheel.

Prince

Oh where is a prince, what can that be,
some venturing locus sick on the sea
chariot feather, swan-y down wing
scarlet his cheeks, eyes dark serene,

Oh, now I believe he is near, yet nowhere seen,
and space is but illusion, trickery of the mind.

the robin
flies to me with fey eyes, he dances from
over the sea.

gossamer are branches at my window,
trickling autumn rain from
ebony nib.

Oh where is that prince who played on golden sky,
a lyre of fire he carries,

One wan look disturbs my soul,
piercing me true
changed forever more,
and it throws me over.

Lucky Horse

I swam in waters distant as pearl
bound my fingers with sand wave curl
deeper still I ventured far
I found a fallen star
crossing through splashing foam
born of great blue roam
twitching in the saline ether
a lucky horse, Pegasus
of sea
lucky sea horse,
lucky me.

Astral House

A thousand storms swim round my heart
I am through desolate mysticism meaning renewed.

The Novel

Onyx autumn night,
a scrying in my soul,
Cool under stone in icy ground
centuries unturned,

Awakens without warning
with one solemn, piercing stare,
I only stand with book in hand,
my fingers marred with ink,

Imploring with my fervour delirium
I beg of it, Speak!
Tell of the things you see
living mysteries to me —

For shadowed silt of ego comes often, washed
by waves of Night, pressing cold fingertips
into my forearms moments before dawn,
when I am at most
alchemical
apex of the hour,
My very consciousness afloat
in Mercury's transmutation
Imploring for the wisdom
of nocturnal sages from centuries unturned.

Passing on the dawn to a forest floor,
a mist crosses inside
optics clear and transient
as the trickling mountain stream,

I know this void is linked somehow,
glassy obsidian obelisk
reflecting more moonlight than I ought
think fair, on the silvery frame
where it sits,

But will it show me what I desire,
my barren thoughts dare hope
to feel some dew or drop or depth
to soothe such inferno.

The darkness at my window sits,
speaking for itself,
and while the works of Fawkes' fire glint,
I return the book to the shelf.

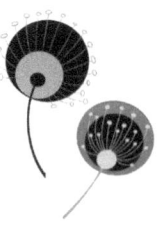

Let Be

Forest green, never seen
Cornwall in December
tangled in the misty coast
where country kisses sea

Breathless like the train
striking at the windy west
seamless like the arrow
piercing my chest

the grass and sky don't turn me on today
just remind me of a home that feels
so far away

Let it shine, let it shine on me
shine,
on me

Can I be sure of what I feel
flying when my mind is still
Silent while my heart still sighs
a pebble cast in pond of night

Cars go quiet as the hills
dressed in fog for miles
something in the distance
A star begins to rise

Dizzy and Such

Close the door so silently
Left a note beside the key
In the garden buried by
the lane

Slipped out through the
neighbour's gate,
tripped against a twist of fate

gem of other realm
exists beyond space
time another matter
for someone else's place

Jazz is cool, heartbroken
strings working inside out
the underwater shapes
A fluttering dawn

Gold-rimmed tea glass
David Bowie
lookalike

The morning I left a
frozen Manhattan
he was already gone.

Mephistopheles

Twisted braids
Slumbering mouth
Trained by the forest
to be wild

I want to camp inside
Your eyes like owls
No one has to know

A situation for another
knotted oak
Midsomer echo
In my mind
While glassy flakes
like stardust rake
The crystal vase
of my spine

Incubus, you're a shiver
I just can't shake
You are the door
then the window
I just can't place

The way
you make me feel
A bit surreal
like Gene Kelly
in the Rain,
I want to see you again

Bloody trees
what do they see
Are you a man or
what man ought to be
A mouth to speak
of all these things
Does your body do the deed when mind speaks hell
Can you tell the
book from spell

Eblis, you're a shiver
That I just can't shake
You are the door
Then the window
I just can't place
The way
you make me feel
A bit surreal
Like Gene Kelly
in the Rain
I want to see you again.

Chimera

What is this
hydra and flame, epoch
cindering dead bits,

A Vision seeping, a Garden seedling,
a Fountain weeping,

the most phosphorescent pearl crown is lost somewhere
down there in the cellar,
on the other side, a boat kisses
the sun through the waves.

New Year Eve

Shudder in shade, your pastel bondage
took a trip to wonder at all the little things
Down by the water
The people of boats
live a different life there,
drawn by the ether, His painting of me,
Threads of smoke shiver
up through my throat
      Signals of fire erupt in my heart.

I want to give it meaning
Open your eyes it says
Look at the world around you
There is nowhere beauty
cannot make her home,

I rise with the moon, frostbitten
by the eve of New Year
trailing what I saw down there
All the little things

A pleasure
your acquaintance Lady Cygnet,
your neck an hourglass,
I gave my hand to a man of stone,
rising from the grass.

Teeth of Kore

So soon you come so soon
watchful flower
then to where do you go
trailing seven moons

and on whose watch do you claim
sundered breath,
stuck steady in smoking window
where all her backward glances are kept,

gigantic ocean these promises kept,
After seeing them all she leapt
to Fate's knees, bring what it will
better to leap than forever stand still.

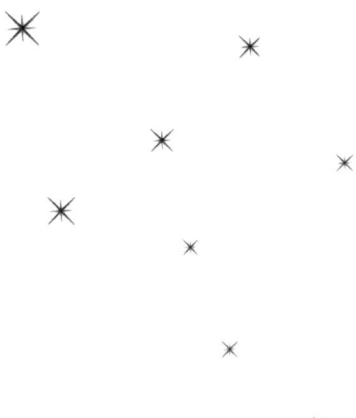

Chalice of Artemis

The hunter's emptiness,
let it come, it will not destroy you
nor me. Though its vividness
may seem a splinter in the effulgence
Of our moon
it is not the kind to use in trade
to buy whatever you see.

It is the chrome of the mirror, showing
yourself for what you really are,
at times strong, others weak

but always traveling, like the huntress,
always seeking, guided by the
sharp scent a moment beyond your circle,
always clever, so clever
you know your traps like the back
of your bow
and they glint, alloy in the moonlight.

Kaleidoscope at 1.33 AM

You say one does not know what dream it is exactly
that causes a tear to fall
from the dreamer's eye
by glow of backward hour—but I
I know.

Sister Poppy

My love, don't go
don't make me face
a Paris hotel alone,
Was I such a fool to rely
On a philosopher's stone.

Shadows of love,
but it wasn't enough
Light threw itself in my eye
off a mirror nearby,

Diamond flood
celestial sight
channeled necromantic Aphrodite
Can't you see the lead in her eyes.

You're from another place
what are you waiting for,
I'd do anything for my knee
to rest your private head.

The Gift of Snow

No more poems in the green room
No more laughter in the hall
tufted bed surreal against
flattened iron sobs

knowing unknowing it is a fracture we blame
the slick Montmartre streets where she asked me my
name
I turned my back to you at the hour
fixing my eyes on the crowds lit afar
Ride a white wolf, fly
winter rider
breathe as a child
delicate as a flower.

Echo Country

Born at the exact same time of day as my mother
Grace is the name of a girl
in L A U S A
waving at the surfers all day

I look down to see the cliffs, another country now
Do what excites.
    Blessed like the Northern Star
    Rising in Echo Country
    Think of your first love.

Echo Country, you are
Blooming, bulging, bursting
Like clouds coming and going
Always in love for the first time.

distant, mellow, grassy
effusion of polite mirages boil
what ought to be
winter air

Echo Country, I look down a second time.
The grace is spreading, growing
has covered a true distance,
beneath our hearts.

I understand now, the pain I held
was my breath as I waited
to see tonight's meteor heart,
exploding in the sky

A gift just for me, still floating
I lean over to see,
so much closer to the clouds that
surround without sound,
the bell within.

Electric Wolf

Broke into a dream
the craziest one so far it seems,
I like magnets but I'm averse to
too much electricity.
It will help someday they say,
"God works in mysterious ways"

So I'm looking for a record now
describing all I'm meant to be—
need something new
to help define a personality.

I think I found it in a Brussels bookstore
rose petal scales and timothy grass tales

Like a dandelion blown sideways to France
where you mean to build a house this year.

La Belle au bois dormant

I make not a sound, curl the books round
me. My undercover light adorning white
fastens the pearl to force the Sun ahead,
two steps ahead, always two, ahead.

Your wink so construct, bevelled, robust,
travels twenty centuries
winds around my ear.
And thus, we, plaited gemstone braves
shrug and
live again.

Rorschach

Bewitched Eye, from afar you cast
cinema of inner doubts
Unseeing clear morning walls
you find the story your seething heart is seeking.

A framed glass, casting spell of the girl
your very inner transformation knows,
her long, chestnut hair, and stockingeyed arms
slender pinned with a big black satin bow.

You discover you know her better than
you might let on,
from a photograph picked by your own
searching.

Is it any wonder your fever
meets its puzzle now.

When you finally rise
to obtain best glimpse
of this scene, so ominous

You find it is not the vision your inner Eye sought,
nothing more than a clouded ink splotch
drawing, a print of a girl, but with an old-fashioned
bow, and her hat is rather charming,
in entirety the actual effect is
disarming.

I'm Your Alien

There are whispers of truths
moving silently through
All we need do is allow.

Ondine

There is a house, it sits asleep next door
with glassy eyes of eternity in its windows,
and when I cross its path
oh, how blankly do they stare,

But I know, yes I know,
What I hear in the night,

How clear
it comes to me

Through the walls, vanished epochs call —

Ondine, I wait for you still
This weight of longing binds me
Ondine, your hair of silk
Has struck me to this prison
with its lightning —

I lean my ear against
the pale of plaster
Wonder, what could this fishing soul pine for,

and how he hides away,
in poplar tower
Crowning windless flame,
burns between
these walls,

Of men and minds we seek to find,
in curiosity we play

Never knowing wooded peaks
we walk towards,

Never do they sway
to hidden emerald shapes,

Ondine, means she came from the sea,
how I'd love to ask him how
All I know is what I hear at night
Ondine, means he waits patiently
won't you set him free with your lightning.

Child of a Psychic

Because I was once forgetful and following
and following—
and forgetful,
sitting near the fire, it was warm
and hurt,
bands of color, expanding in everything
discreetly displaying stories of time, gentle time, this is the way I
    feel:

slowly, like dawn,
spreading my fingers across the table,
watching the red table in Soho, a sort of hospital,
looking for ash to panegyrize.

Not Quite Eight

It is not quite eight, in bed all the same
the way I am trained, because mom and dad say.

still light feels sickly, watered down dusk,
washed away day, nowhere to play
because all the bulbs switched off.

I am not quite eight, I switch on my own,
game in my head, with no-one around,

I leave it a little space,
to warm, settle deep in
cover and sheet, where
cashmere pink heats my cheek,
I discover something new is worked in my play,
settle myself to hear what it says,

Space is, space is dizzy like calm,
float beyond my Self, climbing ladders of sounds,
voices almost, voices almost,
what do they say, energy trickles,
until I can adjust its river,
memorize its frequency,
portcullis of ambrosia.

I'm flying to Paris, it is not quite eight.

Mind

Your eyes trained on mine
crystals in my hair
your face feels the same
called by any name,

The wind blows by
The sea rolls by
and the letter in my hand
catches fire

Once upon a wintry night
I came upon ladies dressed in thunder
and they danced for the pyramids
and they danced for the child
and the words of their voices
were insatiable

Black Cabinet

There is a black cabinet
it heard the vest, enamoured by the
breast of the owner,
who wore him, close to her heart
—golden and rare they were
in the lambent looking glass
set in enamel of black cabinet—

who heard him weep in black night
pressed between the other sheaths
of tumbled cotton velvet shorn
crushed and hung in long straight lines.

Six

Six o'clock so far away,
curtain breathing, sunken
eyelets sing, love can never stay.

A heart has been broken
weeping red dragged under French streetlight,

Two boys share a cigarette, will never let
the girls know what it feels like,

but there is one, a mind its own
when it comes to love,
because Love is all it knows.

Moth

There is a moth beating at my window
    Who will let it in—
Its wings tossed from the moon
carry forgotten things

There is a moth it courses savage
at my head and chamber warm
and all my body moves
to hear it come again so soon—
    oh moth

I hear a moth, its waking skin
powder wings that sing to touch
I hear it keenly, yet is it so
its torment is beauty shivering.

wicked moth you frighten me,
In the night I cannot see,
the moon is low you are covered so
go and let me, let me be.

I know you are patterned grey and smart
to charge right through the limpid heart,
but please take pity this I beg
Leave me in my lying head.

You beat again the metal screen
Finally, I look up,
you are caught between netting
and pane of glass to keep you out,
All to bring me news of night,
while I tempt you with indoor light.

Gypsy Boy of the Darro

Your copper coin for a lovely rose
A black-eyed beauty said to the gypsy boy
She laid her wares against
his painter fingers
Sending her letters by the moon of the Darro

Crowds of flowers dance the hills of the
mountain
All grow pale beside the ones she holds

Many seasons have passed through Darro
mountain
But his love for her is one restless wind

When the troops came in
It was his choice to stay
Her heart was torn away, taken by
the bird of her kin
Never knowing if she would see
her one true love of the Darro
again.

The restless wind is his love
so many years apart not enough
to ease the truth of what could have been
in a war where souls become absent.

Inverness

Sleeping sermon comes
from the dawn,
delivering hymns of the
green-winged things

they called you so far North

No place like home, the faerie trail
sings,
you will find it in your heart.

Does it seem both near and far,
A mineral from the past,
Smoky quartz and clear topaz
ringing Caledonian trees,

Their amber skin, the faultless sky
Should I go or wait,
bearing breath of buried lore,
seamless binding marigold Tor,

Follow where
the felted stag fetches
Mossy crag where
free wind blows.

Bodies of Storm

Desperation for new languge framed by storms greater than avalanches, barreling leaves plastered to skinny legs. I mark my lip where a Spirit stood, pinned by a feather dropped from the sky. She came from Avenue D in some isolation corner with wooden floorboards. I tie my hair back where the snow can hit my neck to remind me of the Vampire who comes to me at Night, every night—

    Hotel lobbies frangipani bodies
    Asway, all asway today
    Preternatural streams
    These strands bend but never break,

    Far from you, closer to me
    Exotic metropolis paler than King
    Stronger than rings
    These strands bend but never break,

    I know the robin song, I know.
    the donkey's hobbling ridge, I count the
    footprints like the dewdrops
    These strands bend but never break.

Cosmo Flora

The natural outpouring of emotion in Nature
results in the perfume of crushed grass
dispelling notions of isolation in the
scent of recreation
where sunlight washes you clean.

Climb the winding dandelion stalk
Lick the gossamer-haired leaves
Observe that trundling amber-shelled fly
Balanced at the crossing of two narrow blades.

Duel

The cost of every bluff, a sound you could place your hand upon,
a scope you could scrape your boots upon like the dust,
like the,
joke you whispered in the shelves of a cotton quilt paired with the
    stilts
of a clock who paired its time with illness
begging in the aisles,
sighing for the skies.   skyways

limitless the rooms they made, burgeoning the men they
swayed looking for a lass, seventy two would come to pass
while all along still six remained both kind not lies,
still born with skies

Such fragmentary penchants, I like your hair
did I mention,
it kind of leaves me when I go from room to room,
a memory is just as good if soon
you'll make one for me,
you'll make one for me,

The boy slammed the book to erase what he had seen,
the girl cuts the eye from the back of the magazine,
they get close and teach each other
words they both can read,
of things and what they mean.

Work

I worked at wood chopping. I worked at wood gritting. I worked at splitting my time in two cities. I love your warehouse, your gentle wall. I love that cedar spells my name, O hallowed marshal. I love the keys broke by books
give me,
in pubs and beds and smoke. I know your gait,
your cold routine, I know your First Letter tied to spleen. I know your bursting rage
kept by the late

Western saddles, by Kerouac, Ferlinghetti, and yes, all of their pussy. I know the murder, the rusted rape, the filthy wanderings, the blietzkrieg finality, I know the Union made by two doves in the alcove we gave to the chapel last century. I know the fair ring of ghosts set on someone's cascading forehead and I, fortunately, have bled to know yet one thing more.

I believe in the sun and the moon more often than not and the rot of the grass is sweeter in July, promises sweeter than any far flung oil on the avenue where thoughts are betrayed by the hind lings of the watchman's dog the night after a raid

Hothouse Flower

Hot house flower steamed
variant bracts implore streaked glass
many footed colours stoop down from rafters
round wooded columns, reaching
for boiling letterbox

A letter from whom, they whisper
in the next brown room; is he tall
or does he draw, is he masked
and does he ask, what annual mood might
peck your pane of crystal view

Ice clay pallor
will he wander
through the fog to find
your petals bright though waterlogged
doubtful by design

then will he touch or want it much,
the frozen-limbed and
green-eyed bunch

Perhaps hour of verdant throne will creep
through burst glass at last
florets beguiling frostbit chiding,

fresh breath coarse pricked
trails of vespers faint breaking.

Kataware-doki means Twilight

listen to your body. it is harmonising emotions.
alchemical hourglass is what Woman is.
heaven is within us, you can see it in twilight.
kataware-doki is thread connecting souls
woken in the mist, the hour
where sunlight falls to moon.

Naked in the Spaniard Inn

Strawberry heart, shyer than the moon
Your closet holds such heavy bones
But I would ride a firefly to break through bars
you've built to stay inside

Wisdom of a stranger's face, vanishes
in wake of electricty trading places with fading daylight,
the sun went down on a garden scene.

Flickering bulbs hang from branches
like pregnant grapes of Dionysus
their arms reaching for the tables
jealous of the lovers' smiles,

I leave the glass alone
Thirst instead for the beauty of the nakedness of
a night in London alone,

Swallow my pride to look inside
a fragile road to roam
burns like desert
drowns like rain
until you can meet what you create, looks like a key
to things awaiting.

oh, Croatia

train tipping the night, I slept across from
your silent mouth in our empty carriage
we spoke not a word, your long hair was black
your father blessed our journey in a language
I could not understand,
as fireworks sent us from Zagreb to Split.

Carte blanche

Let me run to your arms
Oh you who know me so well
All my bruises, and all my books
You who see I'd rather be
in the shadow of the Crow
than reflecting some admirable sun
You who put the dark feather
on the border of my room so I wouldn't
feel so alone,

You chariot, you romantic,
washed upon the shores of Liberty,
to take black coffee in diners,
just take me back inside these walls,
where, I can be reminded
there is always another day

I am your Pilgrim, your Tearaway,
coattail lit by firefly.

Tangerine Oak

Orange rind binding horizon
Your deathless stare, your swallowing omen
Bricks of Lovers fleeing The Storm
restoring falsification of Form

Garnering turpitude, your glance like a knife,
your chandelier wisdom
your Berlinese strife

An oak that confounds you
in bark and in branch
in stoutness it haunts
in veil will advance

Changeless,
this vision of form
Staunch in your raging,
      quaintly you perform her,

Oak that is fleeting, oak so fixed
gazing upon your paired
remittances

Saturn sits high over all, strong in its longing
its pulling digs the weeds
with botany scullery
strange how its song, seems like ironing of belfry,
iron its bond speared by visions of valour,

If you dare, to care
Well you'll melt, your frozen ears

you will pierce the frame you've made
to make room for what you've saved

And if you chance to catch a breeze
that is strong, and that will leave you with hope
of times to come

Ode to Sensitives

What of trust
the steel eye that looks upon
the wool of a lamb,
Is it two legs
stood as sticks
in the garden of the Moon,

Tell me, and what of trust
Can it lie, as the blanket does
when the wind edges in its corners,

what of trust, when the air
that fills the room is even not enough.

But tell me, one thing more, tell me,
what of love.

Does it dry its gaze on the riverbed,
when the waves remain splashing,
does it lean inside bodies
that are hollow like bookshelves,
does it iron their creases
like maidens, who grow candlelight
by digging for change,

Nothing more than a star
that flickers once
in the distance and then it is gone,

it is fleeting but it is real.

Witch

One single finger leaning
lingering light on your lips
You can't tell if
that busy taste you're dragging
is blood or maybe wine or what
You've never been so ignorant
to the sense that navigates
what you long for
and what you despise,

She must have really got you
How you chased her up the stairs
then what could it be, dragging your lids
back down
Heavy as the sand
Relentlessly sharing itself
with the better half
Of a glass shaped like
her body
mocking you from the only window in that
little room of shadows,

You keep confusing them with her,
until you're talking to yourself,
don't worry darling, she
instigates, lifting the latch with that one finger
I'll go and get some help.

Wolfish

Cavernous and queer, those eyes that
stare, and they stare and they stare
and they stare,
and a strange, ringing bell peals a tone
rare and clear, and its clear, clear as
day, clearer still.

Wonder what the wolf would say, if
he talked, as he walked
through his wood at night.
I'd ask him what he's got in there, in
that big shaggy head, on his path, in the dark
and I'd stare.

www.ingramcontent.com/pod-product-compliance
Lightning Source LLC
Chambersburg PA
CBHW030604020526
44112CB00048B/1223